THE
SLIME BOOK

Published by Passageway Press, an imprint of FB &c Ltd. London.
Company number 08720141.

www.PassagewayPress.com

Cover design by Michelle Freer

ISBN 978-1-334-99911-6

First Edition

TABLE OF CONTENTS

INTRODUCTION

Growing up, I used to *beg* my mom to let me make slime. Our homemade recipe wasn't anything fancy, but I could play with that simple slime for hours on end.

As an adult I was super excited when I saw slime surge in popularity again a couple of years ago. I started experimenting with DIY slime recipes with my girls, focusing on taste-safe slimes that my youngest daughter could enjoy worry-free.

Wouldn't you know it - those slime recipes turned out to be the most popular posts on my blog last year!

My best blogging friend (we co-own the kid food blog InTheKidsKitchen.com) Jennifer shares a love of slime, and creates lots of recipes too. She specializes in unique glue-based slimes, and her fluffy slime recipe practically broke the internet last year!

As we traded slime stories, we both came to the realization that we needed to put our brains together and create the ultimate slime resource. That's how *The Slime Book* was born.

Slime has been a way for both of us to spend hours of quality time with our kids. It's an easy set-up activity that can be done indoors or outdoors. No special skills required! (But you might get a tad messy at times!)

I hope you enjoy trying these recipes as much as we enjoyed creating them!

STACEY
TheSoccerMomBlog.com

I started making slimes with my daughter once she was safely out of the "tasting phase". Slime is a great addition to well-rounded sensory play - along with outdoor time, kitchen time, play dough, water play, sensory bins, etc.

I've learned the hard way that vinegar is the best way to remove slime from hair, clothing or carpet. We avoid major messes by playing with slime in areas that are easily cleaned. There's nothing saying you can't take the slime outside or into the bath tub!

Slime is a wonderful sensory play material, but do it at your own pace. I only make slime about twice a month, and I have clear rules so that I'm not scraping slime off the ceiling. It's been great for encouraging my daughter's love of science and is a great stress reliever after a crazy day at school.

You can also use slime to complement other educational subject matter - check out our space slime, rolling a rainbow slime activity, or knead some number beads into your slime!

JENNIFER
SugarSpiceAndGlitter.com

IMPORTANT SLIME SAFETY TIPS

✓ Follow recipes carefully. Slime recipes often involve chemical reactions, with specific ingredients chosen to "activate" the reaction. Substituting can change the reaction, creating new substances that may irritate the skin, or even be dangerous. Even something seemingly innocent like substituting one type of glue for another might have unintended results. Plus, some glues and detergents are actually toxic (we stay away from those!)

✓ Limit exposure to slime and wash hands thoroughly afterwards. Many substances that are safe for use on our skin (soap, for example) could be irritating if left in contact for a long time. Limit the amount of time spent playing with slime and always clean hands well immediately afterwards.

✓ Always supervise! Even if a slime is "safe" or non-toxic, large clumps might still pose a choking hazard to little ones, so make sure you keep a close eye on the play.

✓ Protect surfaces. Always play with slime on a protected surface to prevent damage to furniture, or at the very least, a mess.

✓ While some slimes are noted as "edible" and/or "taste-safe," none of these recipes are intended to be consumed in large amounts or as food items.

✓ If there is any sign of irritation, discontinue use immediately.

✓ If a child ingests any slime that is not noted as "edible" or "taste-safe," contact poison control.

PART 1

CLASSIC SLIMES

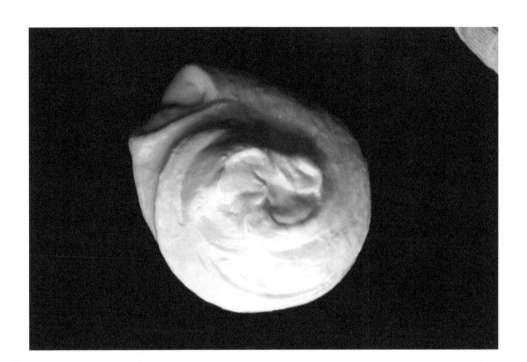
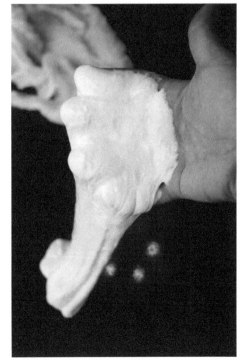
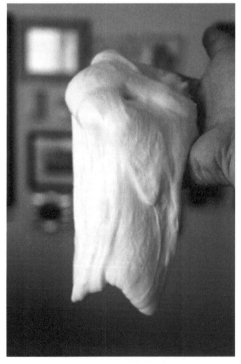

GLUE SLIME

This is the classic recipe for stretchy, squishy glue slime.

INGREDIENTS

1 bottle (5 oz) white school glue

1 teaspoon baking soda

1 tablespoon contact lens solution

Food coloring (optional)

TIP:

Classic glue slime is the basis for lots of other fun slime recipes and projects. It can be customized with glitter, food coloring and more.

DIRECTIONS

1 Add entire bottle of white school glue to a mixing bowl. (Skip generic brands of glue, as they don't always work as well.)

2 Add baking soda to bowl and stir to mix. If using food coloring, add at this time.

3 Add contact lens solution and stir with spoon until slime clumps together. Finish mixing by hand.

4 If slime is still sticky, add another splash of contact lens solution.

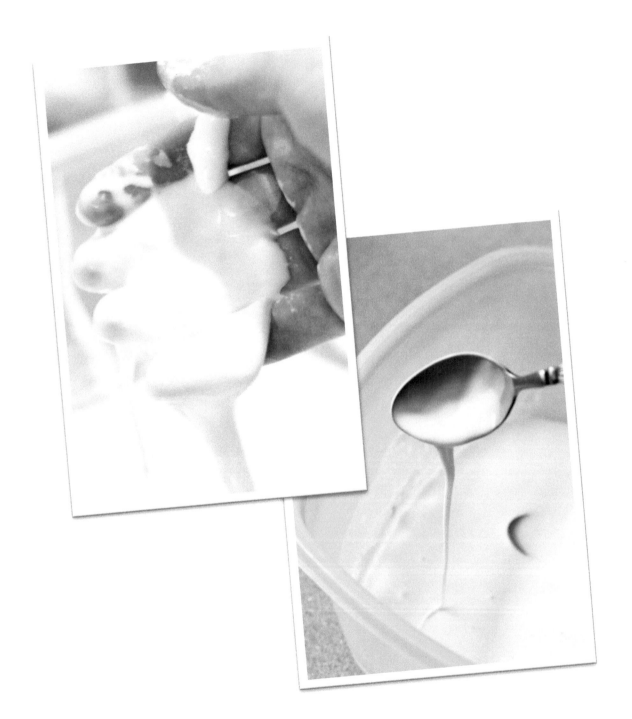

OOBLECK

Is it a liquid? Is it a solid? It's oobleck! A timeless slime recipe for generations.

INGREDIENTS

2 cups cornstarch

1 cup water

Food coloring (optional)

TIP:

We like to add figurines in our oobleck, hiding them and rescuing them from the quicksand-like tub!

DIRECTIONS

1 Add 2 cups cornstarch and 1 cup water to a large mixing bowl and stir until well combined. Mixture will still be watery.

2 Add the second cup of cornstarch little by little until the oobleck begins to thicken up. Stop when you've reached the perfect consistency – solid when you hit it hard with your fingers and liquid if you touch it gently. Amounts may vary slightly depending on whether you like your oobleck more liquid or thick.

3 Add food coloring after you've made your oobleck and watch the colors swirl!

NOISY SLIME

Just like the stuff that everyone loved in the 90's!
Stretchy, squishy, and makes lots of silly noises when you play!

INGREDIENTS

1 cup glue

½ cup water

2 tablespoons contact solution

4 cups shaving cream

2-3 tablespoons borax solution

Food coloring, optional

TIP:

Your slime should be stretchy, squishy and fluffy – and make lively popping noises when it's squeezed, slapped or ripped it half.

DIRECTIONS

1 Start by making a borax solution. Mix ½ cup hot water with ½ tablespoon borax and stir to dissolve. Set aside to let cool before you add it to the slime mixture.

2 In a separate mixing bowl, combine the glue, water and shaving cream. Fold together with a large spoon until completely incorporated. Add any food coloring if using, and mix well before adding in the contact solution.

3 Add the borax solution 1 tablespoon at a time – do not add more than 4 tablespoons total. Stir each tablespoon in well and watch how the slime reacts before adding more.

4 When the slime starts to form a cohesive ball and pulls away cleanly from the bowl, you may begin kneading the slime with your hands. Knead it for at least 2 minutes – if it's still sticky, add a bit more of the borax solution.

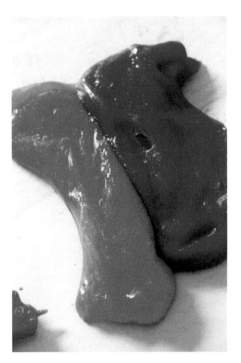

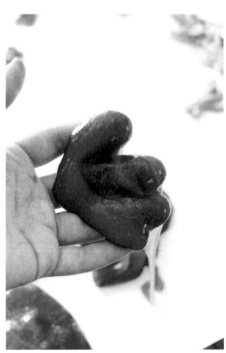

SPARKLY UNICORN SLIME

Perfect for the unicorn-obsessed, this slime can be customized with your favorite sparkly colors. Just don't skimp on glitter!

INGREDIENTS

1 cup pink glitter glue

1 cup purple glitter glue

1 cup liquid starch (can use 10 tablespoons of contact solution instead)

1 tablespoon each of purple and pink glitter

TIP:

Layer pink & purple glitter slimes in a Mason jar and top with plastic unicorn figurines for a gift-able Unicorn Slime

DIRECTIONS

1 Place the pink glitter glue in a bowl and add in the pink glitter.

2 Stir ¼ cup of liquid starch (or 3 tablespoons of contact solution) into the glue.

3 Knead for 2 minutes, adding in more starch or contact solution as needed to make a non-sticky slime.

4 Repeat with the purple glitter glue, purple glitter and remaining slime activator.

5 Twist the two slimes together for lots of glittery fun!

ORANGE FIBER SLIME

Only 2 ingredients, super-stretchy, and taste-safe –
this is one of our favorite easy slime recipes!

INGREDIENTS

1 tablespoon psyllium husk or Orange Metamucil

1 cup water

TIP:

If using a fiber powder, make sure that it includes psyllium husk in the ingredients.

DIRECTIONS

1 Combine the Metamucil and water in a LARGE microwave-safe bowl.

2 Whisk for 1 minute to get it really frothy.

3 Place in microwave for 5 minutes, stopping the microwave whenever it looks like it's going to bubble over the edge.

4 Stir well for 30 seconds, then let sit to cool.

5 When the slime is cool, knead and play!

NEBULA SLIME

Perfect for your star-gazer, this nebula-inspired slime is a great way to dive into the topic of outer space.

INGREDIENTS

1 cup glue

3 - 5 tablespoons contact lens solution

Pink, orange, and yellow food dye

Star glitter

Planet models or marbles (optional)

DIRECTIONS

1 Place glue in a bowl and add 3 tablespoons of contact solution to start.

2 Stir and then knead once incorporated, adding more contact solution as needed.

3 Divide into 3 bowls and add pink food dye to one, orange to the second and yellow to the third. Stir to incorporate.

4 Lay the slime in rows next to each other and sprinkle on the star glitter and planets, as desired.

5 Stretch, squish and explore your own piece of outer space!

PART II

HOLIDAY SLIMES

JANUARY — SNOW SLIME

A fun way to transform slime - pop it in the freezer!

INGREDIENTS

One batch of glue-based slime

Silicone ice cube container

TIP:

Add characters or small toys to extend the fun - we added little penguins for an iceberg party.

DIRECTIONS

1 Divide slime into sections of your ice cube container or muffin tray. (We used a silicone heart muffin tray.)

2 Freeze for 2 hours or until ready to play.

3 Pop the frozen slime out of the container and start playing.

4 Notice the differences the slime goes through as it transitions from a solid, frozen slime to hard, yet squishy shapes, back to its original slime state.

FEBRUARY — CONVERSATION HEART SLIME

A classic stretchy slime with a Valentine's Day surprise!

INGREDIENTS

1 cup glue

3 - 5 tablespoons contact solution

Pinch baking soda

½ cup conversation hearts

TIP:

For a fun pastel effect, break up some of the conversation hearts and mix the powder into the slime.

DIRECTIONS

1 Place glue and 3 tablespoons contact solution in a bowl and stir well. Add a pinch of baking soda and knead.

2 Add more contact solution as needed to get a consistent, not sticky, texture.

3 Knead in the conversation hearts.

MARCH — RAINBOW SLIME

Follow the rainbow to a pot of gold!
This rainbow of different colored slimes eventually turns into gold as you play!

INGREDIENTS

1 cup clear glue

¼ - ½ cup liquid starch, as needed

2 drops food coloring (per color)

Generous sprinkle of glitter

Splash of water

TIP:

St. Patrick's Day-themed Invitation to Play: add pretend gold coins, shamrocks, etc.

DIRECTIONS

1 Divide glue into 6 containers. Add 1 tablespoon of liquid starch and a few drops of water to each bowl, along with food dye. Dye one bowl each color: red, orange, yellow, green, blue, and purple.

2 Knead for 2 minutes, checking consistency and balancing with more glue or more liquid starch as you go.

3 After you have a cohesive slime add any optional coloring, glitter, sequins, and scent.

4 Set each color of slime aside as you make them: red, orange, yellow, green, blue and purple.

5 Roll out a "snake" of each color and line up together in a rainbow.

APRIL — BIRD SEED SLIME

Celebrate Spring with bird seed slime!

INGREDIENTS

1 (8oz) bottle clear glue

3-6 tablespoons liquid starch

1 tablespoon water

1 cup bird seed

Bird figurines

TIP:

You can use this method of making slime for a confetti slime, perler bead slime, rock slime, or just about anything where you want to add texture.

DIRECTIONS

1 Place glue in a large bowl.

2 Add in bird seeds and stir to combine.

3 Add in 3 tablespoons of liquid starch and stir 1 minute after completely incorporated.

4 Test the consistency and add more starch as needed until the slime is not super sticky.

5 Pick up and knead for 2 minutes, adding more starch as needed to reduce the stickiness.

MAY — FLOWER SLIME

Warm weather and blooming flowers call for flower slime!

INGREDIENTS

1 cup glue

¼ - ½ cup liquid starch (may substitute
5 tablespoons contact lens solution)

1 cup small fabric flowers

TIP:

Swap out the flowers for different seasons - white and red poinsettia-style flowers for winter, autumn leaves or fall-colored flowers for fall, etc.

DIRECTIONS

1 Place glue in a bowl and add in ¼ cup of liquid starch and when a cohesive ball of slime forms.

2 Start kneading in your flowers until you have as many flowers as you desire.

3 Knead for 2 minutes, adding in more liquid starch as needed.

JUNE — SUNSHINE CITRUS SLIME

Celebrate summer solstice with this bright glitter slime that smells like sunny citrus fruit!

INGREDIENTS

1 bottle (5 oz) orange glitter glue

⅛ cup baking soda

⅛ cup contact lens solution

5 drops orange essential oil

TIP:

Feel free to use any citrus oil that you have on hand: grapefruit, lemon, etc.

DIRECTIONS

1 Pour entire bottle of glitter glue in mixing bowl.

2 Add baking soda, contact lens solution, and essential oil and stir until slime forms. Finish mixing by hand.

3 If slime is still sticky, add another 1 teaspoon of contact lens solution.

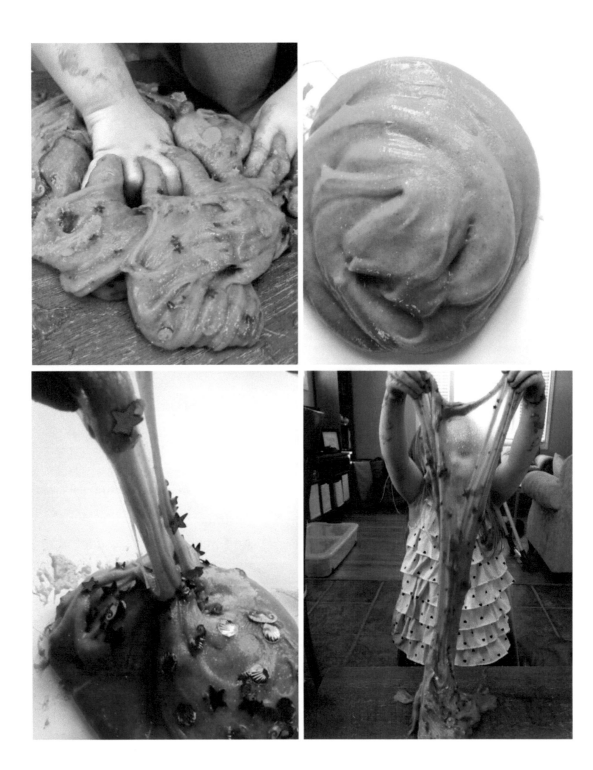

JULY — MERMAID SLIME

**Take a vacation with this sparkly mermaid slime!
Perfect for indoor sensory play on hot summer days.**

INGREDIENTS

1 cup clear glue

¼ - ½ cup liquid starch, as needed

2 tablespoons water

¼ teaspoon teal gel food coloring

Generous shake of teal glitter

Mermaid glitter or sequins

TIP:

Craft stores are a great place to find special types of glitter and confetti for all occasions!

DIRECTIONS

1 Mix the glue, ¼ cup of liquid starch, and water together to start.

2 Knead for 2 minutes, checking consistency and balancing with more glue or more liquid starch as you go.

3 After you have a cohesive slime, add any optional coloring, glitter, sequins, and scent.

AUGUST — SNOW CONE SLIME

This snow cone slime looks like the real thing and has a fun crunchy texture!

INGREDIENTS

1 cup glue

¼ - ½ cup liquid starch (can use 5 tablespoons of contact solution instead)

1 cup small aquarium pebbles, or more as desired

Red and blue food dye

TIP:

This slime might look delicious, but it is not edible.

DIRECTIONS

1 Place ⅓ cup of glue in a bowl, add in ⅓ cup of aquarium pebbles, or more as desired.

2 Add in 1 tablespoon of contact solution or ¼ cup of liquid starch.

3 Stir until a cohesive ball starts to form.

4 Add more slime activator (starch or contact solution) to achieve a non-sticky slime.

5 Repeat with the remaining ingredients, dying one bowl blue and one bowl red before starting to knead.

6 Place all three slimes side by side in a plastic cup and have fun playing with your crunchy snow cone slime.

SEPTEMBER — APPLE PIE SLIME

A taste-safe slime flavored like apple pie candy!
You might even have everything you need to make it in your kitchen right now!

INGREDIENTS

1 (14oz can sweetened condensed milk)

½ cup cornstarch

1 teaspoon cinnamon

Dash apple flavoring or apple pie spice

TIP:

If slime starts to get sticky, simply add a touch more cornstarch, or coat hands.

DIRECTIONS

1 Place the sweetened condensed milk and 1 tablespoon of cornstarch in a saucepan over medium heat.

2 Stir constantly for 5 minutes until the milk takes on a caramel color and starts to thicken.

3 Remove from heat and fold out onto a cutting board dusting with cornstarch.

4 When the mixture is cool enough to handle, knead more cornstarch into it until you achieve a not sticky texture.

5 Add cinnamon and apple flavoring as desired.

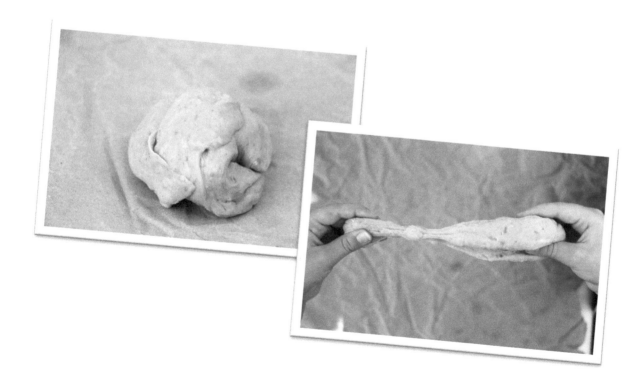

OCTOBER — HALLOWEEN CANDY SLIME

A fun way to use up extra Halloween candy! This edible slime has a thick, putty-like texture.

INGREDIENTS

½ cup chewy Halloween candy (taffy, Starburst, etc.)

⅛ cup confectioner's sugar

⅛ cup cornstarch

TIP:

If slime hardens, simply microwave for a few seconds to soften.

DIRECTIONS

1 Unwrap candy and place in a microwave safe bowl. Heat for 20 seconds, 10 seconds at a time, stirring between.

2 Remove from microwave and add powdered sugar and cornstarch. Stir until mixture thickens.

3 When mixture is too thick to stir with a spoon, finish kneading by hand. *Careful, make sure slime has cooled enough to handle first!*

NOVEMBER — PUMPKIN SEED SLIME

This pumpkin seed slime perfectly recreates the goo inside a real pumpkin!

INGREDIENTS

1 cup clear glue

½ cup liquid starch, or as needed

2 tablespoons water, if needed

Orange food coloring

Clean pumpkin seeds

TIP:

Adding pumpkin scent or some pumpkin spice takes this recipe to the next level!

This slime is not edible.

DIRECTIONS

1 Place glue in a large bowl

2 Add in pumpkin seeds and stir to combine.

3 Add in 3 tablespoons of liquid starch and stir 1 minute after completely incorporated.

4 Add orange food coloring and stir to mix.

5 Test the consistency and add more starch as needed until the slime is not super sticky.

6 Pick up and knead for 2 minutes, adding more starch as needed to reduce the stickiness.

DECEMBER — CRANBERRY SLIME

Only 2 ingredients and completely edible!
This wiggly slime is perfect for the holidays or any time of year

INGREDIENTS

1 cup cranberry sauce

1 cup cornstarch, plus extra as needed

TIP:

You can adjust the amounts of cranberry sauce and cornstarch to whatever you like — as long as it's equal parts.

DIRECTIONS

1 Place the cranberry sauce in a bowl and work out or remove some of the large clumps with a spoon.

2 Add an equal amount of cornstarch and stir well. It will get increasingly hard to stir and you may need to start using your hands to knead it together. Add more cornstarch as needed to get a not-sticky, dough-like texture.

3 Store in the fridge when not in use.

PART III

EDIBLE SLIMES

GELATIN SLIME

This taste-safe slime changes colors as you mix it!
An easy recipe that washes right off with soap and water.

INGREDIENTS

½ cup cornstarch

½ large package gelatin

2 tablespoons water + more as needed

TIP:

For mess-free play, pour your gelatin slime into a plastic zipper bag and seal

DIRECTIONS

1 Pour cornstarch and gelatin powder in a medium mixing bowl and stir well.

2 Add 2 tablespoons water to dry ingredients. Stir until a paste begins to form. (Your mixture will begin to turn a vivid color!)

3 Continue to add water a tablespoon at a time until the slime clumps together instead of sticking to the bottom/sides of bowl.

CHOCOLATE PUDDING SLIME

A cross between slime and play dough, this edible chocolate pudding slime closely resembles a certain infamous emoji character.

INGREDIENTS

1 cup cornstarch

½ of a 3.4 oz package chocolate instant pudding mix

⅓ cup warm water

Edible candy eyes

TIP:

If slime begins to dry out, simply add a splash of water and work into the dough until it re-hydrates.

NOTE

It is perfect to style to look like the poo emoji.

DIRECTIONS

1 Combine instant pudding mix and ⅓ cup cornstarch in a medium mixing bowl.

2 Add ⅓ cup warm water and whisk with a fork until a smooth pudding forms. If there are a few small lumps that is ok; they will work out later.

3 Add another ⅓ cup of cornstarch and stir until well mixed.

4 Add remaining ⅓ cup cornstarch and finish mixing by hand until slime no longer sticks to skin.

GUMMY BEAR SLIME

Who knew gummy bears could do THIS?! A stretchy, marshmallow-like slime that smells amazing and tastes delicious.

INGREDIENTS

1 cup gummy bears

2-3 tablespoons icing sugar

2-3 tablespoons cornstarch

TIP:

Feel free to substitute any type of gummy candy you have on hand.

NOTE

This slime is not reusable.

DIRECTIONS

1 Heat the gummy bear slime in the microwave for 10-15 seconds, stir, and reheat as necessary to break down the gummy bear shape.

2 Knead in your icing sugar and cornstarch in equal amounts, until the gummy bear slime forms a cohesive dough/slime consistency. The more you add, the less sticky the slime will be – but also the more you add the thicker and less stretchy it will be.

STARBURST SLIME

This is a fun STRETCHY slime that has its roots in the old-fashioned practice of "pulling taffy." Also doubles as a great "fondant" substitute for baking.

INGREDIENTS

20 taffy candies, unwrapped

3-5 tablespoons icing sugar

TIP:

This slime gets less stretchy the more it's played with but it can be safely reheated and played with again.

DIRECTIONS

1 Count out about 20 candies for a "single serving" of this slime recipe.

2 Place a saucepan or double boiler filled with water on the stove over high heat, and allow to come to a boil as you unwrap your candies.

3 When the water is boiling add the candies to a glass bowl over the boiling water (or to your double boiler) just a few at a time. I found it was easier to get a few starting to melt and then add more in, rather than adding them all at the same time.

4 Once the candies have lost their original shape and are forming a thick dough, continue cooking and stirring for about 2-3 minutes to thin out the mixture, being careful not to burn your candies.

5 Fold the melted candies out onto a cutting board with 3 tablespoons of icing sugar. Allow the taffy to cool until you can comfortably touch it.

6 Knead the icing sugar into the melted taffy until it's not sticky, adding more as needed.

FUDGE SLIME

An easy edible chocolate slime recipe that smells just like your favorite decadent desserts!

INGREDIENTS

½ cup cornstarch

1 tablespoon cocoa powder

⅓ cup coconut milk

TIP:

If dough seems to dry out, heat in microwave for about 10 seconds. This softens the coconut cream in the recipe and brings back the slime texture.

DIRECTIONS

1 Add heaping ½ cup of cornstarch and 1 tablespoon cocoa powder to a medium mixing bowl. Whisk together until well combined and you have a light brown powder.

2 Make sure to use a microwave-safe bowl and handle with care. Heat ⅓ cup coconut milk in microwave until warm (not steaming or boiling). This should take about 20 seconds.

3 Pour warm coconut milk into mixing bowl with cornstarch and cocoa powder. Milk together with a spoon until a smooth slime begins to form. You'll be able to easily scoop the putty out of the bowl by hand when you're done mixing.

FROSTING DOUGH

This Birthday Cake Batter Edible Play Dough smells good enough to eat!

INGREDIENTS

1 part white frosting

3 parts cornstarch

1 tablespoon water

Sprinkles (optional)

TIP:

If the batter is still sticky, continue adding cornstarch a spoonful at a time until you have a soft, moldable ball of dough that does not stick to hands.

DIRECTIONS

1 Start by combining about a teaspoon of your cornstarch with water in a medium mixing bowl. Stir until cornstarch is fully dissolved in water.

2 Add your frosting to the bowl and stir a couple times. Add the rest of your cornstarch little by little until the mixture clumps together to form a batter. As it thickens it may be easier to mix with your hands to better incorporate the ingredients.

YOGURT SLIME

Smoothy & stretchy, great for all ages!

INGREDIENTS

1 cup yogurt

¾ cup cornstarch

TIP:

Yogurt slime becomes more oobleck-like the more you play with it so we recommend playing over a bowl or container.

DIRECTIONS

1 Place yogurt in a large bowl and stir to break down any lumps.

2 Whisk or stir in your cornstarch - the slime will eventually get too tough to stir and you will need to knead with your hands.

3 Knead until the slime is cohesive, wetting your hands if it's a bit crumbly.

4 Add a couple drops of food coloring for extra fun!

EDIBLE HONEY SLIME

The kids will be buzzing about this sweet and stretchy new slime recipe!

INGREDIENTS

¼ cup honey

¾ cup cornstarch

1-2 tablespoons oil

TIP:

If slime starts to harden, simply heat for about 5 seconds to soften it right up!

DIRECTIONS

1 Heat honey for 45 seconds in the microwave (be sure to use a microwave safe bowl and handle with care, as bowl may become hot).

2 Add the cornstarch 2 Tablespoons at a time until completely incorporated into the honey. When you can no longer stir with a spoon, finish kneading by hand (check to make sure that slime is cool enough to handle comfortably).

3 Add the oil, as needed, until the slime is stretchy and not sticky.

MARSHMALLOW "FOAM" SLIME

Who needs a stress-relief ball with this fluffy sensory play!

INGREDIENTS

½ cup cornstarch

½ large package sugar free flavored gelatin

2 tablespoons water + more as needed

1 cup mini marshmallows, or more as needed

TIP:

We aim for a ratio of ⅔ marshmallows to ⅓ slime. This gives the foam a bouncy, fluffy texture.

DIRECTIONS

1 Pour cornstarch and gelatin powder in a medium mixing bowl.

2 Add 2 tablespoons water to dry ingredients. Stir until a paste begins to form. (Your mixture will begin to turn a vivid color!)

3 Continue to add water a tablespoon at a time until the slime clumps together instead of sticking to the bottom/sides of bowl.

4 Add a cup of mini marshmallows to the bowl. Stir with a spoon until marshmallows are coated in slime.

5 Finish mixing by hand.

PEANUT BUTTER SLIME

This soft and malleable peanut butter slime is just like the lunchbox staple
(except it won't stick to your hands!)

INGREDIENTS

2 tablespoons creamy peanut butter

1 tablespoon light corn syrup

1 tablespoon cornstarch, more as
needed

TIP:

If you have allergy concerns, feel free
to substitute another type of nut
butter or even sunflower seed butter.
You may need to add more cornstarch
if your substitute is runnier in
consistency than a typical peanut
butter.

DIRECTIONS

1 Start by whisking together peanut butter
and corn syrup until smooth.

2 Gradually add about a tablespoon of
cornstarch, stirring as you go, until slime
starts to form.

3 If your peanut butter slime sticks to
hands, add a touch more cornstarch.

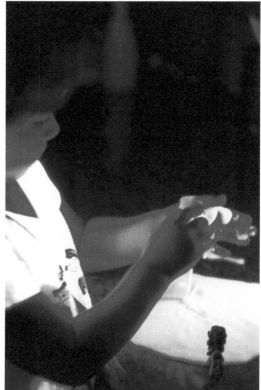

EDIBLE GLOW-IN-THE-DARK SLIME

Take your homemade slime to the next level with this groovy glow in the dark slime recipe!

INGREDIENTS

1 ½ cups cornstarch

¾ cup tonic water

1 cup marshmallows (melted)

TIP:

If you prefer more of a liquid oobleck, use less cornstarch. If you prefer a thicker, dough-like slime, use more cornstarch.

DIRECTIONS

1 Combine ½ cup corn starch and ¾ cup tonic water. Whisk together until well combined.

2 Place 1 cup small marshmallows in a microwave safe bowl and microwave 20-30 seconds, stirring halfway through. Remove from microwave and spoon into your mixing bowl where you're making slime. (Use caution, as bowl may be hot).

3 Whisk marshmallows into your mixture until smooth.

4 Add remaining cup of corn starch little by little, stirring as you go, until you reach your desired consistency.

5 Turn on a blacklight for glowing fun!

PIZZA SLIME

Tastes and smells just like the delivery classic!

INGREDIENTS

¼ cup pizza sauce

2 ounces smooth processed cheese (like Velveeta)

7 tablespoons cornstarch

TIP:

This slime can be stored in an airtight container in the fridge for 2-3 days. Simply knead to soften the slime (your body heat will warm it back up!)

DIRECTIONS

1 Place 2 ounce block of Velveeta cheese in a microwave safe bowl. Heat for 10-15 seconds until soft.

2 Add ¼ cup pizza sauce to bowl and stir to combine. It's ok if the mixture is still a bit lumpy at this point.

3 Add 3 tablespoons cornstarch to bowl and whisk until smooth.

4 Continue adding cornstarch, one tablespoon at a time, until the pizza slime no longer sticks to the sides of the bowl (about 7 tablespoons total).

5 Finish kneading by hand.

EDIBLE BIRTHDAY CAKE SLIME

This fluffy slime smells just like a fresh-baked cake and tastes amazing too!

INGREDIENTS

2 cups marshmallows

3 tablespoons coconut oil, as needed

1 teaspoon vanilla extract

1 - 1 ½ cups powdered sugar

Sprinkles (optional)

TIP:

Keep extra oil for lubricating hands while playing - this will help prevent slime from sticking.

DIRECTIONS

1 Melt the marshmallows in a microwave-safe bowl in 30-second bursts, then stir well to ensure it is fully melted.

2 Stir in 1 tablespoon coconut oil plus the vanilla extract until well combined.

3 Add the powdered sugar in ¼ cup increments, stirring well in between each addition.

4 Finish kneading the powdered sugar into the slime by hand.

5 Add up to 2 tablespoons oil to lubricate the slime and make it nice and stretchy while preventing it from sticking to your hands.

EDIBLE MERMAID SLIME

Super-stretchy and taste-safe, this vibrant blue slime is the color of the ocean!

INGREDIENTS

1 tablespoon psyllium husk (clear)

1 cup water

2-3 drops teal food coloring

TIP:

Add edible starfish or seashell candy sprinkles for more under-the-sea fun!

DIRECTIONS

1 Combine the psyllium husk, water, and food coloring in a LARGE microwave-safe bowl.

2 Whisk for 1 minute to get it really frothy.

3 Place in microwave for 5 minutes, stopping the microwave whenever it looks like it's going to bubble over the edge.

4 Stir well for 30 seconds, then let sit to cool.

5 When the slime is cool, knead and play!

PART IV

UNIQUE SLIMES

3-INGREDIENT FLUFFY SLIME

One of our most famous recipes! This thick, squishy slime has taken over the internet!

INGREDIENTS

1 cup glue

3 cups shaving cream

5+ tablespoons contact lens solution

TIP:

This slime needs a scientific attitude when you're making it - it can take some adjusting and time to get it just right but you'll get it there and have a blast when you do!

DIRECTIONS

1 Empty glue into a large bowl with your choice food coloring.

2 Start adding in the shaving cream. It will continue to get thick and puffy.

3 Next, add in the contact solution. Add ½ cup of solution at a time and then start adding smaller amounts towards the end. The contact solution serves as your "slime activator."

4 Keep stirring with your spatula and adjust as needed.

5 Once the slime is cohesive, no longer sticky or appearing to have any liquid in the mixture, start kneading the slime - this is going to help it be less sticky (just like making homemade play dough).

6 Knead the slime for at least 3 minutes before adding any more ingredients to adjust.

7 When the slime has been thoroughly kneaded and adjusted, give it to the kids in a clean, wide-open area that you don't mind getting a little messy.

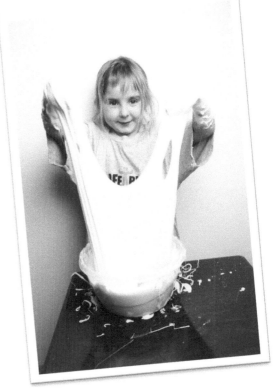

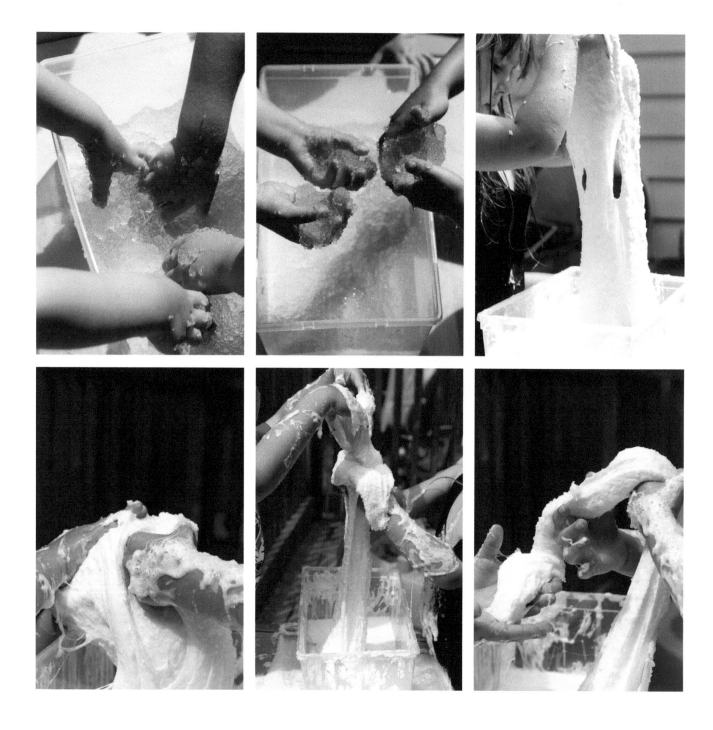

DIAPER SLIME

A great way to use up (clean) diapers after kids have outgrown them.

INGREDIENTS

5 cups water

2-3 cups liquid starch (approximate)

3 - 3 ½ cups white school glue (approximate)

4 disposable diapers

TIP:

This slime recipe makes a TON of fluffy slime so it's great for a crowd.

If you don't have diapers handy fluffy bath crystals can be used instead.

DIRECTIONS

1 Cut open the diapers and shake the diaper crystals out from in between the cotton layers - they will look like little grains of salt - and place in your slime container.

2 Add your water and let the crystals hydrate.

3 Slowly add in 3 cups of glue and then add in the liquid starch.

4 Stir until completely combined, then knead the slime until it's not sticky anymore.

5 Add more glue or starch as needed.

HOT COCOA SLIME

A delicious smelling slime perfect for when the cold weather arrives.
Marshmallows optional.

INGREDIENTS

1 cup glue

½ cup liquid starch, as needed

2 tablespoons cocoa powder, or more

Mini marshmallows, optional

TIP:

The glue will slowly melt the mini-marshmallows as you play. This is a (safe) chemical reaction at play!

DIRECTIONS

1 Combine the glue and ¼ cup of the liquid starch. Stir well.

2 Add in the cocoa powder and knead into the slime.

3 Add in more liquid starch as needed until the slime is no longer sticky. Knead for at least a minute in between additions.

4 Sprinkle on marshmallows, if desired, and enjoy.

POLKA DOT SLIME

This polka dot slime can be customized in so many different ways - changing out the color of the pom-poms or adding food dye to the slime. Think "team colors" or inspired by a special character.

INGREDIENTS

1 cup glue

½ cup liquid starch (can use 5 tablespoons of contact solution instead)

1 cup pom-poms

Food dye, optional

Glitter, optional

TIP:

We love switching this up for special occasions - red slime with green pom-poms for Christmas, orange slime with black pom-poms for Halloween, etc.

DIRECTIONS

1 In a bowl, combine your glue and pom-poms.

2 Add in ¼ cup of liquid starch and when a cohesive ball of slime forms, start kneading.

3 Knead for 2 minutes, adding in more liquid starch as needed.

CRUNCHY GLOW IN THE DARK SLIME

You can make this slime crunchy by adding in glow-in-the-dark pebbles, or enjoy it as a silky smooth slime.

INGREDIENTS

1 cup glue

½ cup liquid starch (can use 5 tablespoons of contact solution instead)

1 teaspoon glow in the dark acrylic paint

½ cup glow in the dark pebbles, optional

TIP:

Try the bathtub to contain any mess when playing with this slime in the dark.

DIRECTIONS

1 Place the glue in a large bowl and add in the glow in the dark paint.

2 Stir well to combine, then add in half of the glow pebbles, if using.

3 Add in the slime activator - either ¼ cup of liquid starch or 3 tablespoons of contact solution.

4 Knead for 1 minute and then add in more pebbles, as desired.

5 Add in more slime activator as needed to get a smooth, not sticky, slime.

6 Be sure to place the slime in the sun or direct light before bringing into a dark place to watch it glow!

 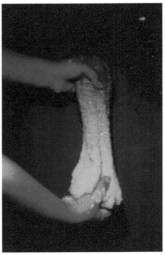 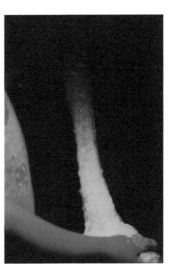

BUTTER SLIME

Use a commercial kids' modeling clay for this slime that spreads and stretches smooth as butter. (This slime is not edible).

INGREDIENTS

1 cup glue

1-3 cups of shaving cream, optional

5+ tablespoons contact lens solution, or as needed

½ cup air dry modeling clay

TIP:

This slime can be made without shaving cream for a less "puffy" version. It hardens with time so shape it into a slime sculpture when you're done playing.

DIRECTIONS

1 Empty your glue into a large bowl. Add glitter or food dye as desired and stir it in.

2 Start adding in the shaving cream. We emptied most of our 283g shaving cream canister into the slime mixture - but just keep adding until you don't feel like there is any "just glue" left. It will continue to get thick and puffy.

3 Next, add in the contact solution. We added it in slowly, but we ended up using an entire bottle so you can definitely add ½ cup of solution at a time, and then start adding smaller amounts towards the end. The contact solution serves as your "slime activator."

4 Keep stirring everything with your spatula and adjust as needed.

5 Once the slime is cohesive, no longer sticky or appearing to have any liquid in the mixture, start kneading the modeling clay into the slime.

6 You will end up with a moldable, stretchy and silky feeling slime.

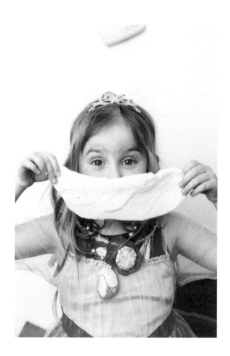

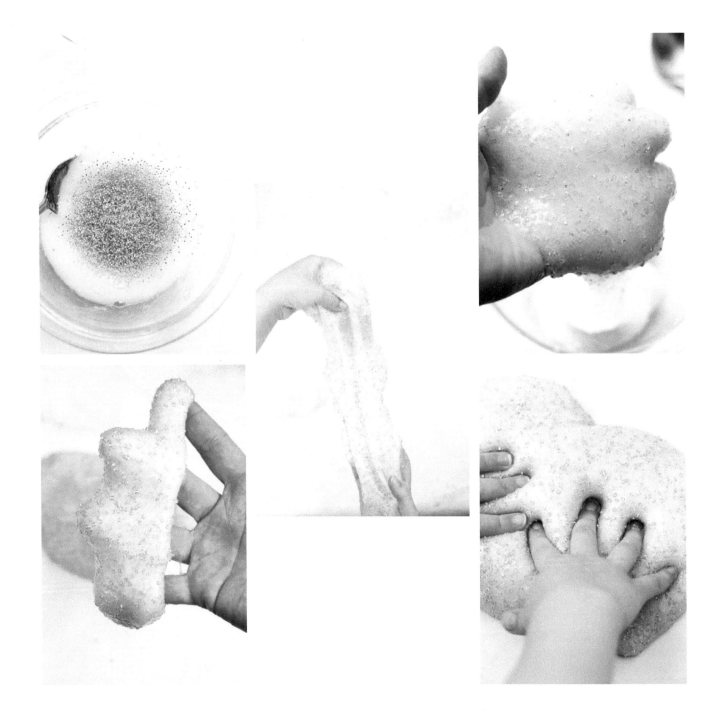

CINDERELLA SLIME

Sparkly, blue, and crunchy like ice!

INGREDIENTS

1 cup glue

3-5 tablespoons contact lens solution, or as needed

½ cup glass microbeads

TIP:

The microbeads may fall out of this slime as you play with it so we recommend playing over a tray to capture the loose beads.

DIRECTIONS

1 Combine the glue and microbeads until you reach a saturation level you like.

2 Add in the contact solution and stir until slime starts to form.

3 Knead the slime for 2 minutes, adding more contact solution as needed to reduce stickiness.

SAND SLIME

This slime can be made two ways - fluffy or just stretchy. This is the fluffy version (omit shaving cream for stretchy).

INGREDIENTS

1 cup glue

3 cups shaving cream

5+ tablespoons contact lens solution, or as needed

½ cup sand, as needed

TIP:

You can use just about any sand for this recipe - sand from the beach, sandbox, or even colored craft sand.

DIRECTIONS

1 Combine the glue and sand until you reach a saturation level you like.

2 Add in the shaving cream and mix until fully incorporated.

3 Add in the contact solution and stir until slime forms a dough-like texture.

4 Knead the slime for 2 minutes, adding more contact solution as needed to reduce stickiness.

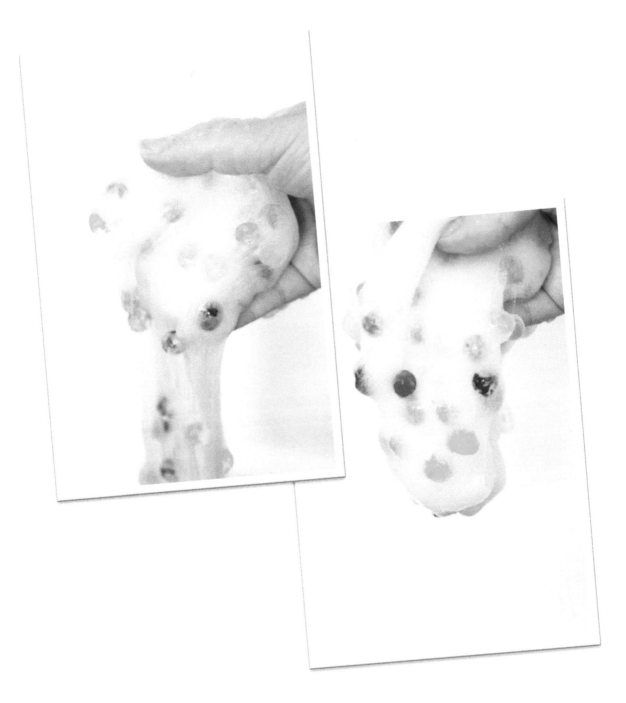

WATER BEAD SLIME

Stretchy and slippery water bead slime is a textured sensory play experience.

INGREDIENTS

1 cup glue

½ cup liquid starch (may substitute 5 tablespoons contact lens solution).

1 cup hydrated water beads (¼ teaspoon dehydrated)

TIP:

The water beads will try to escape your slime - just knead them back in. Playing over a container will prevent the water beads from rolling away.

DIRECTIONS

1 Place your water beads in a cup of water and set aside to hydrate. This may take up to an hour.

2 When the water beads are fully hydrated, drain out the excess water and start making your slime.

3 Place your glue in a separate bowl and mix in ½ cup of water beads, adding more as desired.

4 Add in ¼ cup of liquid starch and when a cohesive ball of slime forms, start kneading.

5 Knead for 2 minutes, adding in more liquid starch as needed.

SLIME DRAWINGS

A fun way to play with slime - draw on it!
Stretch out your drawings and draw new things over and over.

INGREDIENTS

1 batch of white slime

Markers

TIP:

The slime will eventually take on a colorful tie-dye effect.

DIRECTIONS

1 Make a plain batch of white slime. (1 cup white glue, ½ cup liquid starch and a splash of water)

2 Stretch out the slime and gently draw on with markers. I found that making small dots with the markers was easiest.

3 Notice how the slime pulls and reacts to your drawings.

4 Stretch out and knead to start over.

BUBBLE SLIME

A fun, new way to play with slime - blowing bubbles! This is a thinner slime that is great for crafts after you're done with the bubbles.

INGREDIENTS

1 ½ cups of glue (we used 2 6oz bottles)

1 tablespoon hand lotion

1 tablespoon water

15 pumps foaming hand soap

½ cup shaving cream PLUS 1 handful extra

2-4 tablespoons liquid starch

Food dye and/or glitter optional

TIP:

This slime lasts for up to a week in a tightly sealed container (keep at room temperature)

DIRECTIONS

1 Empty your glue bottles into your mixing/storage container.

2 Add the water, mix well, then the hand lotion and mix well.

3 Add 5 pumps of the foaming hand soap at a time, stirring each addition in before adding more.

4 Add the food coloring and foaming shaving cream and completely mix.

5 Add the liquid starch slowly - 1 tablespoon at a time and stirring well in between each addition. Watch how your slime forms with each addition - you want it to be cohesive and pulling away from the sides of the container.

6 Knead the slime well for at least 2 minutes. You can play with it for a while before moving onto the next step.

7 When you are done kneading/playing with the slime, place it back in the container and cover with a handful of the shaving cream (covering the top completely).

8 When ready to play, remove the lid and dig in! To make the bubbles, insert a straw into the slime and blow. The bubbles are super stretchy and can be touched.

CPSIA information can be obtained
at www.ICGtesting.com
Printed in the USA
LVHW050111051218
599172LV00018B/550/P